Book Outline: "The Time Transformer: Crafting Your Path to Success"

By Jenny Koo

Table of Content

Introduction

- Importance of productivity in daily life
- Introduction to time management planners
- Overview of the 10 productivity hacks

Chapter 1: The Foundation of Productivity

- Significance of productivity
- Introduction to time management
- Overview of planners as effective tools

Chapter 2: Goal-Setting Power with GoalGetter

- Exploring GoalGetter
- Effective goal-setting strategies
- Habit tracking for progress
- Celebrating wins and monthly reviews

Chapter 3: Structuring Success with Daily Doen

- In-depth look at Daily Doen
- Comprehensive daily planning
- Balancing work and personal tasks
- Gratitude journaling for positivity

Chapter 4: Dream Big with Visionary

- Visionary planner exploration
- Utilizing the vision board feature
- Long-term planning for big ideas
- Fostering creativity with abundant space

Chapter 5: Wellness and Mindfulness

- Wellness Warrior: Tracking health and wellness
- Encouraging healthy habits
- Mindful Maven: Living mindfully
- Mindfulness exercises and self-care

Chapter 6: Superheroes of Planning

- Time Titan: Time blocking for efficiency
- Taskmaster: Prioritizing tasks effectively
- Efficiency Expert: Boosting overall productivity
- Real-life efficiency success stories

Chapter 7: Holistic Approaches

- Balance Builder: Achieving work-life equilibrium
- Reflection Rookie: Personal growth and reflection
- Self-reflection, goal setting, progress tracking
- Real-life stories of balance and growth

Conclusion

- Key takeaways from each productivity hack
- Reinforcing the importance of planning

Appendix

- Glossary of technical terms
- Additional resources for further reading

Introduction

- Importance of productivity in daily life
- Introduction to time management planners
- Overview of the 10 productivity hacks

Introduction

In our fast-paced world, where time is both a valuable resource and a constant challenge, mastering productivity becomes essential for a fulfilling and successful life. This introduction lays the groundwork for your journey into "Time Mastery: Your Guide to Real Results in 2024," providing a friendly and easy-to-understand exploration of the core concepts.

Importance of Productivity in Daily Life

Why does productivity matter in our day-to-day existence?

Productivity is like the engine that propels us forward in our daily endeavors. It's the secret sauce that transforms dreams into reality, helping us achieve more, stress less, and find fulfillment in what we do. Think about a day when you've effortlessly checked off all your tasks – that feeling of accomplishment and satisfaction is what productivity brings to our lives.

Introduction to Time Management Planners

What are these magical tools, and how can they revolutionize the way we manage our time?

Time management planners are your personal assistants in the journey of mastering time. They're not just notebooks; they're strategic allies designed to help you navigate through the chaos of your daily schedule. Picture them as your roadmap, guiding you through tasks, goals, and aspirations. They're about more than just jotting down to-dos; they're about intentional living and purposeful choices.

Overview of the 10 Productivity Hacks

What's the secret sauce?

Imagine having a treasure chest of powerful techniques that can significantly impact your daily life. These are the 10 productivity hacks we're about to explore. Each one is like a unique tool in your productivity toolbox, ready to be unleashed to transform the way you approach your goals, tasks, and overall lifestyle. From goal-setting power to structuring success, and even holistic approaches, these hacks cover a spectrum of strategies tailored to make 2024 your most productive year yet.

With this introduction, you're not just embarking on a journey; you're stepping into a realm where productivity becomes your ally, not a daunting task. Let's dive in and uncover the secrets to mastering time for real results in 2024!

Chapter 1: The Foundation of Productivity

- Significance of productivity
- Introduction to time management
- Overview of planners as effective tools

Significance of Productivity: Why it Matters in Daily Life

In our busy lives, productivity is more than just staying busy; it's about achieving meaningful results efficiently. Let's explore why productivity matters and how it transforms our daily experiences.

Introduction:

Productivity isn't about being busy for its own sake. It's the secret sauce that turns your efforts into tangible outcomes, providing a sense of purpose and accomplishment.

Why Productivity Matters:

Productivity allows you to accomplish more in less time, leaving space for personal growth, relaxation, and satisfaction. Picture a day where you efficiently tackle tasks, experience accomplishment, and still have time for activities you enjoy – that's the power of productivity.

Example:

Consider a student during exams. Effective time management involves prioritizing tasks, focusing on impactful study sessions, and ensuring breaks for rest. The result? Academic success and a balanced life.

In Everyday Terms:

Productivity is like having a superhero sidekick – guiding you through challenges, ensuring every action contributes to your success and well-being.

Conclusion:

Understanding the significance of productivity is the first step to unlocking its potential. It's about intentional choices, finding balance, and realizing that productivity is more than a buzzword – it's the key to a fulfilling and accomplished life.

Introduction to Time Management

In the hustle of our daily lives, managing time effectively becomes a game-changer. But what exactly is time management, and how does it empower us to navigate the complexities of our schedules?

Cracking the Code of Effective Time Management:

Time management is the art of making the most of the 24 hours we all have each day. It's not about squeezing in as many tasks as possible; it's about making strategic choices that align with your priorities. Think of it as the compass that guides you through the labyrinth of your daily schedule, ensuring you reach your goals without unnecessary detours.

Why Time Management Matters:

Effective time management allows you to work smarter, not harder. It's about prioritizing tasks, setting goals, and allocating time wisely. Picture planning a road trip – time management involves setting goals (your destinations), prioritizing (choosing scenic spots), and staying focused on your journey, ensuring you reach your destination efficiently.

Example:

Consider a professional juggling work, family, and personal goals. Effective time management involves setting realistic priorities, dedicating focused time to each aspect, and ensuring that all areas of life receive attention without feeling overwhelmed.

In Everyday Terms:

Time management is your personal GPS, guiding you through the twists and turns of your day, helping you avoid traffic jams (time-wasting activities), and ensuring you reach your destination (goals) efficiently.

Conclusion:

As we explore time management, remember that it's not about fitting more into your day; it's about making intentional choices that bring you closer to your priorities. Effective time management is the key to achieving more while maintaining a sense of balance in your life.

Overview of Planners as Effective Tools

In our quest for mastering time, planners emerge as indispensable tools. But what elevates a simple planner from a collection of pages to a strategic ally in our daily lives?

Planners: More than Paper and Binding:

Planners are not mere notebooks; they are your personal assistants in the journey of mastering time. They provide structure, aid in goal-setting, and keep you on track. Think of them as the architects of your day, helping you build a solid foundation for your goals and aspirations.

Why Planners Matter:

Planners offer a tangible way to bring order to chaos. They are not just about jotting down tasks; they are about intentional living and purposeful choices. Imagine having a reliable friend who reminds you of deadlines, helps you plan your day, and celebrates your achievements – that's the essence of a planner.

Example:

Consider planning a major event. A planner is like your event coordinator, ensuring every detail is accounted for, deadlines are met, and the overall vision is achieved. It's the tool that turns chaos into a well-executed plan.

In Everyday Terms:

Your planner is your ally, standing by your side as you navigate the challenges of your day. It's the friend who keeps you focused on what truly matters and ensures that each action contributes to your overall success.

Conclusion:

As we explore planners as effective tools, envision them not just as notebooks but as strategic partners in your journey. They are there to provide guidance, structure, and support, helping you make intentional choices and ensuring that your time is invested wisely.

Chapter 2: Goal-Setting Power with GoalGetter

- Exploring GoalGetter

- Effective goal-setting strategies
- Habit tracking for progress
- Celebrating wins and monthly reviews

Exploring GoalGetter

GoalGetter isn't just a planner; it's a dynamic tool designed to elevate your goal-setting and productivity game. In this section, we delve into the essence of GoalGetter, unveiling its unique features and functionalities that make it a pivotal companion in your journey towards intentional living.

Unveiling the Planner's Potential:

Purpose and Beyond:

GoalGetter transcends the conventional role of a planner. It emerges as a strategic partner, guiding you through intentional living. Unlike traditional planners, GoalGetter is crafted to transform your dreams into actionable plans.

Design and Layout:

Explore the thoughtful layout of GoalGetter, combining user-friendliness with powerful functionalities. From goal-setting sections to habit trackers, each element is strategically placed to ensure a seamless and effective planning experience.

Features and Sections:

Goal-Setting Mastery:

Delve into GoalGetter's dedicated sections for goal-setting. It goes beyond a mere task list, providing a structured space to articulate and refine your aspirations. Whether it's professional milestones, personal growth, or health goals, GoalGetter accommodates them all.

Habit Tracking for Progress:

Uncover the habit-tracking feature within GoalGetter. This is more than just logging habits; it's a tool to cultivate positive behaviors. GoalGetter becomes your accountability partner, ensuring you stay on track with your daily routines.

Celebrating Wins and Monthly Reviews:

Discover the significance of the monthly review section. It's not just a routine check; it's a crucial aspect of GoalGetter's design. Learn how monthly reviews help you celebrate wins, analyze challenges, and make necessary adjustments for continuous improvement.

Example: Turning Dreams into Plans

Consider a practical example: let's say your goal is to learn a new language. In GoalGetter, the goal-setting section allows you to break down this ambitious task into manageable steps. You can set specific language milestones, track your daily learning habits, and celebrate achievements like completing a language level. GoalGetter transforms the abstract dream of learning a new language into a tangible, achievable plan.

Exploring GoalGetter in this section is about recognizing its multifaceted capabilities. It's not just a tool for scheduling; it's an intentional living companion that empowers you to take charge of your aspirations. Get ready to unlock the full potential of GoalGetter and turn your goals into reality in 2024.

Effective Goal-Setting Strategies

Effective goal-setting is the cornerstone of achieving meaningful results with GoalGetter. In this section, we explore strategies that go beyond mere aspirations, providing you with a roadmap to turn your dreams into actionable and achievable goals.

The Art of Goal-Setting:

Understanding SMART Criteria:

Effective goal-setting starts with the SMART criteria—Specific, Measurable, Achievable, Relevant, and Time-bound. Dive into each element:

- Specific: Define your goal clearly. Instead of saying "exercise more," specify "run 5 kilometers three times a week."
- Measurable: Establish criteria to track your progress. For instance, track the number of words written daily if your goal is to finish a book.
- Achievable: Set realistic goals to maintain motivation. If you're new to running, a marathon might be too ambitious initially.
- Relevant: Ensure your goals align with your values and long-term objectives.
- Time-bound: Define a timeframe for each goal to create a sense of urgency.

Breaking Down Larger Goals:

Large goals can be overwhelming. Learn the art of breaking them down into smaller, more manageable tasks. This not only makes your objectives clearer but also allows you to celebrate achievements along the way.

Real-Life Application:

Career Milestones:

Suppose your goal is a career promotion. Break it down by setting specific targets, such as acquiring new skills, completing relevant projects, or expanding your professional network. Each accomplished step brings you closer to the overarching goal.

Fitness Objectives:

For fitness goals, apply the SMART criteria. Instead of a vague "get in shape," define specifics like running a 10k in three months, measuring progress by increasing running distance weekly.

Effective goal-setting is about turning abstract dreams into concrete plans. As you employ these strategies with GoalGetter, envision your aspirations taking shape through well-defined objectives and actionable steps. The planner becomes your ally, ensuring each goal is not just a wish but a realistic target you're well on your way to achieving.

Habit Tracking for Progress

Habit tracking within GoalGetter is a powerful tool for cultivating positive behaviors and ensuring sustained progress towards your goals. In this section, we'll delve into the significance of habit tracking, how it works, and why it's a game-changer for building lasting habits.

Why Habits Matter:

The Science of Habit Formation:

Understand the psychology behind habit formation. Habits are the building blocks of our daily routines, and tracking them is essential for introducing positive changes. By consistently engaging in positive behaviors, you reinforce neural pathways, making these habits more automatic over time.

The Accountability Factor:

GoalGetter's habit-tracking feature acts as your personal accountability partner. It's not just about jotting down habits; it's a mechanism that nudges you toward consistency. Knowing you're tracking your habits creates a sense of responsibility, encouraging you to stay committed.

Creating Positive Habits:

Identifying Target Habits:

Begin by identifying habits aligned with your goals. Whether it's a daily writing routine, regular exercise, or mindfulness practices, GoalGetter helps you pinpoint specific behaviors crucial for your success.

Setting Achievable Targets:

Avoid overwhelming yourself. Set achievable targets for habit formation. If your goal is to read more, start with a realistic daily reading time that can gradually be increased. GoalGetter ensures your habit targets are within reach.

Example:

Fitness Journey:

Consider a fitness goal. If your aim is to adopt a healthier lifestyle, GoalGetter's habit-tracking section can include habits like daily workouts, drinking a specific amount of water, or getting enough sleep. Tracking these habits reinforces your commitment to a healthier lifestyle.

Habit tracking isn't just about recording actions; it's a dynamic process of creating positive behaviors that align with your goals. With GoalGetter, witness your habits evolving from conscious efforts to ingrained routines, bringing you one step closer to sustainable progress.

Celebrating Wins and Monthly Reviews

In the journey towards your goals with GoalGetter, celebrating wins and conducting monthly reviews are integral practices. This section explores why acknowledging achievements is crucial and how monthly reviews contribute to continuous improvement and goal alignment.

The Importance of Celebration:

Psychological Benefits:

Celebrating wins, no matter how small, has profound psychological benefits. It reinforces positive behavior and motivates you to keep moving forward. GoalGetter encourages you to pause, reflect, and acknowledge your achievements, creating a positive feedback loop for sustained motivation.

Building Momentum:

Each celebrated win contributes to the momentum of your journey. Whether it's completing a task, achieving a milestone, or cultivating a new habit, these celebrations become milestones that propel you toward larger goals.

Monthly Reviews:

Reflecting on Progress:

Monthly reviews within GoalGetter are more than routine check-ins; they are opportunities for reflection. Assess your progress, evaluate what worked well, and identify areas for improvement. The reflective process provides insights into your journey, helping you make informed decisions for the upcoming month.

Adjusting Goals:

One of the key aspects of the monthly review is the flexibility to adjust your goals. Life is dynamic, and so are your aspirations. If certain goals no longer align with your priorities, this is the time to recalibrate and set new targets.

Real-Life Stories of Growth:

Work-Life Balance Success:

Consider a scenario where your goal was to achieve a better work-life balance. A celebrated win could be consistently leaving work on time. In the monthly review, you might realize that incorporating short breaks during the day positively impacted your productivity.

Personal Development Journey:

For a personal development goal, like learning a new skill, celebrating the completion of an online course could be a significant win. During the monthly review, you might find that dedicating a specific time each day for learning was particularly effective.

Celebrating wins and conducting monthly reviews with GoalGetter create a holistic approach to goal pursuit. It's not just about the destination; it's about appreciating the journey, learning from experiences, and continually aligning your goals with your evolving aspirations. As you integrate these practices, watch your progress unfold in a way that's not just productive but also fulfilling.

Chapter 3: Structuring Success with Daily Doen

- In-depth look at Daily Doen
- Comprehensive daily planning
- Balancing work and personal tasks
- Gratitude journaling for positivity

Structuring Success with Daily Doen: An In-depth Look

Daily Doen is not just a planner; it's a strategic ally in structuring your path to success. This section provides a comprehensive exploration of Daily Doen, shedding light on its unique features and how it facilitates effective daily planning.

Unlocking the Essence of Daily Doen:

Purpose and Functionality:

Daily Doen is designed to be more than a daily scheduler. It's a tool that empowers you to structure your day with purpose. Unlike generic planners, Daily Doen offers a nuanced approach, understanding that each day is a unique journey with its own set of tasks and priorities.

User-Friendly Interface:

Explore the user-friendly interface of Daily Doen. Its layout is intuitive, ensuring that even on your busiest days, you can navigate through your tasks effortlessly. From work-related deadlines to personal commitments, Daily Doen accommodates them seamlessly.

Comprehensive Daily Planning:

Time Blocking for Efficiency:

Delve into the concept of time blocking within Daily Doen. This technique involves dedicating specific blocks of time to different tasks. It's not just about listing what needs to be done but strategically allocating time, enhancing focus, and ensuring productivity throughout the day.

Prioritizing Tasks:

Learn how Daily Doen aids in prioritizing tasks. It's not just about managing your to-do list; it's about discerning between urgent and important tasks. By focusing on high-priority items, you optimize your productivity and make significant strides towards your goals.

Balancing Work and Personal Tasks:

Holistic Task Management:

Daily Doen recognizes the need for a holistic approach to task management. It seamlessly integrates work and personal tasks, acknowledging that success extends beyond professional accomplishments. Balancing both aspects of life ensures a well-rounded and fulfilling existence.

Gratitude Journaling for Positivity:

Cultivating a Positive Mindset:

Daily Doen introduces the practice of gratitude journaling. Understand how taking a moment each day to express gratitude contributes to a positive mindset. This simple yet impactful practice fosters resilience and enhances your overall outlook on life.

Realizing the Power of Reflection:

Gratitude journaling is not just about listing things you're thankful for; it's a form of reflection. Discover how reflecting on positive aspects of your day, whether big or small, contributes to a mindset of abundance and contentment.

In this in-depth exploration, we've peeled back the layers of Daily Doen, revealing its nuanced features that go beyond traditional planning. It's not merely a tool for managing time; it's your companion in structuring success, fostering balance, and nurturing a positive mindset. Get ready to harness the full potential of Daily Doen and make every day a step towards a successful and fulfilling life.

Comprehensive Daily Planning with Daily Doen

Daily Doen is your partner in achieving a holistic and productive day. In this section, we delve into the comprehensive daily planning features of Daily Doen, showcasing how it transforms your day-to-day schedule into a strategic and efficient roadmap.

Time Blocking for Efficiency:

Strategic Time Allocation:

One of the key features of Daily Doen is the practice of time blocking. Understand how this technique involves breaking your day into distinct blocks, each dedicated to a specific task or activity. It's not just about making a to-do list; it's about allocating focused time for each task, enhancing efficiency and minimizing distractions.

Enhancing Focus and Productivity:

Explore how time blocking enhances focus. By dedicating a specific time frame to a particular task, Daily Doen encourages deep work and minimizes multitasking. This intentional approach to time management ensures that each activity receives the attention it deserves, resulting in heightened productivity.

Prioritizing Tasks Effectively:

Urgent vs. Important:

Daily Doen empowers you to discern between urgent and important tasks. Learn how to categorize your tasks based on their significance, ensuring that you prioritize activities that align with your goals and contribute to your overall success. This strategic prioritization maximizes your impact, making your daily efforts more purposeful.

Daily Doen's Priority System:

Discover how Daily Doen's priority system works seamlessly within the comprehensive daily planning framework. Whether using labels, color-coding, or other visual cues, Daily Doen helps you easily identify and focus on high-priority tasks, ensuring that crucial activities take precedence.

Adaptability and Flexibility:

Dynamic Task Adjustments:

Life is dynamic, and so is your daily schedule. Daily Doen allows for adaptability, enabling you to adjust your plan as circumstances change. Learn how this flexibility ensures that you stay in control of your day, even when unexpected events arise.

Integration of Work and Personal Tasks:

Holistic Task Management:

Daily Doen understands the importance of work-life balance. Explore how it seamlessly integrates work and personal tasks, recognizing that success encompasses achievements in both spheres. This integration ensures that your day is well-rounded, catering to both professional responsibilities and personal fulfillment.

Comprehensive daily planning with Daily Doen is about more than organizing your tasks; it's a strategic approach to time management. By incorporating time blocking, prioritization, flexibility, and holistic task management, Daily Doen transforms your daily routine into a well-structured plan that propels you towards your overarching goals. Get ready to embrace a more organized, focused, and productive daily life with Daily Doen by your side.

Balancing Work and Personal Tasks with Daily Doen

Daily Doen recognizes the intricate dance between professional responsibilities and personal fulfillment. In this section, we explore how Daily Doen acts as a facilitator in harmonizing work and personal tasks, ensuring that your day is not just productive but also fulfilling on a personal level.

Holistic Task Management:

Seamless Integration of Work and Personal Tasks:

Daily Doen provides a platform where work and personal tasks coexist harmoniously. Learn how this integration acknowledges that success is not confined to professional achievements alone; it extends to personal growth, well-being, and meaningful connections.

Visualizing Your Day:

Explore how Daily Doen's layout allows you to visualize both work-related commitments and personal activities. By having a comprehensive view of your day, you can make informed decisions, ensuring that neither aspect of your life takes precedence at the expense of the other.

Flexible Scheduling:

Adapting to Your Rhythm:

Daily Doen understands that everyone has a unique rhythm when it comes to productivity and personal activities. Discover how the flexibility of Daily Doen's scheduling allows you to adapt to your natural energy levels, optimizing your work and personal tasks based on your daily rhythm.

Creating Time Blocks for Personal Activities:

Learn how Daily Doen facilitates the creation of dedicated time blocks for personal activities. Whether it's spending time with family, pursuing hobbies, or engaging in self-care, Daily Doen encourages intentional scheduling, ensuring that personal tasks are accorded the time they deserve.

Preventing Burnout:

Strategic Allocation of Resources:

Daily Doen aids in preventing burnout by strategically allocating your time and energy. Understand how the planner prompts you to balance demanding work tasks with rejuvenating personal activities, fostering a sustainable approach to productivity.

Real-Life Application:

Professional Achievement and Personal Well-Being:

Consider a scenario where your professional goal is to complete a challenging project. Daily Doen allows you to allocate focused time blocks for work tasks. Simultaneously, it ensures that personal tasks, such as breaks, meals, and moments of relaxation, are seamlessly integrated. This balanced approach fosters productivity without compromising well-being.

Quality Family Time:

For personal goals, like spending more quality time with family, Daily Doen enables you to set aside dedicated time blocks for family activities. This intentional scheduling ensures that personal aspirations are given the same level of importance as professional goals.

Balancing work and personal tasks with Daily Doen is about crafting a day that reflects your priorities in both realms. By seamlessly integrating these aspects, Daily Doen empowers you to lead a well-rounded and fulfilling life where professional achievements and personal fulfillment coalesce seamlessly. Get ready to embrace a balanced and intentional approach to task management with Daily Doen as your guide.

Gratitude Journaling for Positivity with Daily Doen

Daily Doen goes beyond conventional planners by incorporating a powerful tool for fostering positivity and well-being—gratitude journaling. In this section, we'll explore how the practice of gratitude journaling within Daily Doen contributes to a positive mindset and an enriched daily experience.

The Practice of Gratitude:

Understanding Gratitude Journaling:

Discover how Daily Doen introduces the practice of gratitude journaling—a daily ritual where you reflect on and jot down things you are thankful for. Gratitude journaling is not just an exercise in positivity; it's a mindful acknowledgment of the positive aspects of your life, no matter how big or small.

Realizing the Power of Reflection:

Explore how gratitude journaling is a form of reflection. It encourages you to pause, look back on your day, and identify moments, experiences, or people that brought joy, satisfaction, or growth. This reflective practice contributes to a heightened awareness of the positive elements in your life.

Cultivating a Positive Mindset:

Creating a Positive Feedback Loop:

Understand how gratitude journaling contributes to creating a positive feedback loop. By actively seeking and acknowledging positive aspects daily, you train your mind to focus on the good, fostering a positive mindset that transcends challenges and enhances resilience.

Boosting Mental and Emotional Well-Being:

Learn about the broader benefits of cultivating a positive mindset. Daily Doen's incorporation of gratitude journaling aligns with research indicating that regularly practicing gratitude can lead to improved mental and emotional well-being, reduced stress, and increased overall life satisfaction.

Real-Life Stories of Growth:

Celebrating Small Wins:

Consider a scenario where your goal is to complete a challenging project at work. In your gratitude journal, you might celebrate small wins, like successfully overcoming a hurdle or receiving positive feedback. These acknowledgments contribute to a positive work environment.

Personal Development Journey:

For personal goals, such as adopting a healthier lifestyle, gratitude journaling may include being thankful for nutritious meals, successful workout sessions, or moments of self-reflection. These reflections reinforce positive behaviors and contribute to the overall well-being journey.

Gratitude journaling with Daily Doen transforms your daily planning experience into a holistic practice. It's not just about managing tasks; it's about cultivating a positive mindset that permeates every aspect of your life. As you integrate gratitude journaling into your daily routine, get ready to witness the transformative power of acknowledging the positive elements in your life with Daily Doen as your guide.

Chapter 4: Dream Big with Visionary

- Visionary planner exploration
- Utilizing the vision board feature
- Long-term planning for big ideas
- Fostering creativity with abundant space

Dream Big with Visionary Planner: Exploration

Embark on a journey of boundless possibilities with the Visionary planner. In this section, we delve into the intricacies of the Visionary planner, exploring its features and guiding you on how to utilize this powerful tool to turn your dreams into actionable plans.

Unveiling the Visionary Planner:

Purpose and Essence:

Understand the fundamental purpose of the Visionary planner. It goes beyond traditional planning by providing a space to not only organize tasks but also to articulate and pursue your dreams. Explore how the planner serves as a compass, guiding you towards your aspirations.

Unique Features:

Explore the unique features that set the Visionary planner apart. From specialized sections for long-term goals to creative spaces for brainstorming, the Visionary planner offers a multifaceted approach to planning that accommodates the diverse dimensions of your dreams.

Utilizing the Vision Board Feature:

Visualizing Your Dreams:

Dive into the innovative vision board feature of the Visionary planner. Learn how this tool allows you to visualize your dreams and aspirations through images, quotes, and symbols. The vision board serves as a powerful motivator, providing a daily visual reminder of the bigger picture you're working towards.

Creating a Vision Board:

Practical tips guide you through the process of creating an effective vision board within the Visionary planner. From selecting impactful images to incorporating inspirational quotes, discover how to curate a vision board that resonates with your goals and keeps you inspired.

Long-Term Planning for Big Ideas:

Setting Grand Goals:

Explore the dedicated sections within the Visionary planner for long-term planning. Whether your dreams involve launching a business, pursuing further education, or traveling the world, the Visionary planner provides a structured framework for setting and pursuing grand goals.

Breaking Down Big Ideas:

Learn effective strategies for breaking down big ideas into manageable steps. The Visionary planner encourages a systematic approach, ensuring that each step is actionable and contributes to the realization of your long-term aspirations.

Fostering Creativity with Abundant Space:

Unleashing Your Imagination:

Discover how the Visionary planner fosters creativity with its abundant space for freeform thinking. Whether you're sketching, jotting down ideas, or mind mapping, the planner provides a canvas for your imagination to roam free.

Creativity as a Productivity Booster:

Understand the link between creativity and productivity. The Visionary planner recognizes that fostering creativity isn't just about artistic expression; it's a powerful tool for problem-solving, ideation, and innovation that propels your dreams forward.

In this exploration of the Visionary planner, you'll uncover not just a planning tool but a catalyst for turning your dreams into tangible plans. From the intricacies of its features to practical tips on utilizing its tools, the Visionary planner becomes your companion on the exciting journey of transforming aspirations into reality.

Utilizing the Vision Board Feature of the Visionary Planner

Unlock the transformative power of the Visionary planner's vision board feature as we delve into the intricacies of its utilization. This section guides you through the process of turning your dreams and aspirations into visually compelling and motivating elements within the planner.

Understanding the Vision Board Feature:

Purpose and Significance:

Grasp the fundamental purpose of the vision board feature within the Visionary planner. It serves as a dynamic visualization tool, allowing you to compile images, quotes, and symbols that represent your dreams. The vision board goes beyond words, offering a visual representation that resonates with your aspirations on a deeper level.

Creating a Visual Blueprint:

Learn how the vision board becomes your visual blueprint for success. Whether your dreams are centered around career milestones, personal development, or lifestyle goals, the vision board is a dynamic canvas where you can map out your desires and keep them at the forefront of your daily planning.

Practical Steps in Creating Your Vision Board:

Selecting Impactful Imagery:

Explore the art of selecting images that resonate with your goals. Whether sourced from magazines, the internet, or personal photos, each image should evoke the emotions and aspirations tied to your dreams. Understand how a carefully curated selection enhances the effectiveness of your vision board.

Incorporating Inspirational Quotes:

Discover the role of inspirational quotes in amplifying the impact of your vision board. Quotes have the power to encapsulate the essence of your goals and serve as daily affirmations. Learn how to choose quotes that align with your aspirations and elevate the motivational aspect of your vision board.

Integration with Daily Planning:

Making the Vision Board a Daily Companion:

Understand how the Visionary planner seamlessly integrates the vision board into your daily planning routine. Explore practical tips on making the vision board a constant companion, ensuring that you engage with and draw inspiration from it daily.

Aligning Visual Elements with Tasks:

Learn the art of aligning visual elements on your vision board with specific tasks and goals. The Visionary planner provides a structured approach to connecting your visual aspirations with actionable steps, ensuring that your daily tasks contribute to the realization of your larger dreams.

The Motivational Impact:

Daily Encounters with Your Dreams:

Grasp the motivational impact of encountering your vision board daily. The Visionary planner ensures that your dreams are not confined to distant aspirations but are an integral part of your daily planning experience. This consistent exposure fosters a mindset geared towards actively working towards your goals.

Harnessing Motivation for Productivity:

Understand how the motivation derived from the vision board becomes a powerful productivity booster. It goes beyond traditional planners by tapping into the emotional and visual aspects of goal-setting, creating a heightened sense of purpose and commitment to your aspirations.

Utilizing the vision board feature within the Visionary planner is a dynamic and personal journey. From the careful selection of imagery to the seamless integration with your daily planning, the vision board becomes a tangible manifestation of your dreams. Get ready to infuse your planning experience with inspiration, motivation, and a visual roadmap to turn your aspirations into reality.

Long-Term Planning for Big Ideas with the Visionary Planner

Step into the realm of visionary goal-setting as we explore how the Visionary planner empowers you to plan and execute big ideas. This section is your guide to leveraging the dedicated features within the planner for long-term planning, ensuring that your grand aspirations find a structured and actionable path to realization.

Setting Grand Goals:

Identifying Long-Term Aspirations:

Understand the initial phase of long-term planning—identifying your grand goals. Whether it's launching a business, completing an advanced degree, or achieving a major career milestone, the Visionary planner provides dedicated sections to articulate and clarify these ambitious aspirations.

Clarifying Your Vision:

Explore how the planner prompts you to clarify your vision for each long-term goal. This involves defining the specifics, understanding the motivations behind the goal, and envisioning the desired outcome. The Visionary planner ensures that your big ideas are not just abstract concepts but well-defined objectives.

Breaking Down Big Ideas:

Strategic Division into Milestones:

Learn how the Visionary planner facilitates the strategic division of big ideas into manageable milestones. Each long-term goal is deconstructed into actionable steps, creating a roadmap that transforms daunting aspirations into a series of achievable tasks.

Establishing Realistic Timelines:

Explore the importance of establishing realistic timelines for each milestone. The Visionary planner guides you in setting achievable deadlines, ensuring that your long-term goals are approached with a sense of urgency and accountability.

Aligning Tasks with Long-Term Goals:

Integration with Daily Planning:

Discover how the Visionary planner seamlessly integrates long-term goals into your daily planning routine. The planner serves as a bridge between your visionary aspirations and the practical steps you take each day. Learn how to align daily tasks with the overarching objectives of your big ideas.

Consistency in Execution:

Understand the role of consistency in executing long-term plans. The Visionary planner emphasizes the importance of daily commitment to the tasks associated with your big ideas. Consistent execution ensures that each step contributes to the gradual realization of your grand goals.

Realizing the Vision:

Adapting to Changes:

Acknowledge the dynamic nature of long-term planning. The Visionary planner provides flexibility to adapt to changes, unforeseen challenges, or evolving circumstances. Learn how this adaptability ensures that your planning remains responsive to the ever-changing landscape of pursuing big ideas.

Celebrating Milestones Along the Way:

Explore the significance of celebrating milestones as you progress towards your long-term goals. The Visionary planner encourages acknowledgment and celebration at each stage, fostering a positive and motivating environment for continued pursuit.

Long-term planning for big ideas with the Visionary planner is not just about setting distant goals; it's a strategic and dynamic approach to turning your big ideas into achievable realities. By breaking down grand aspirations, aligning tasks with overarching objectives, and maintaining consistency, the Visionary planner becomes your trusted companion on the journey of transforming visionary dreams into tangible achievements.

Fostering Creativity with Abundant Space in the Visionary Planner

Immerse yourself in a realm of boundless imagination as we explore how the Visionary planner provides abundant space for fostering creativity. This section is your guide to understanding and leveraging the creative potential of the planner, allowing your ideas to flourish and evolve into actionable plans.

Unleashing Your Imagination:

Purpose of Abundant Space:

Delve into the purpose behind the Visionary planner's provision of abundant space. Unlike conventional planners, the Visionary planner recognizes the need for expansive areas that go beyond task lists—spaces where your creativity can unfold. Understand how this freedom of space serves as a canvas for your ideas.

Beyond Traditional Planning:

Explore how the Visionary planner transcends the limitations of traditional planning. Abundant space isn't just about jotting down tasks; it's about providing room for mind maps, sketches, doodles, and any form of creative expression that aligns with your goals. The planner becomes a versatile tool that adapts to your unique thinking process.

Creativity as a Productivity Booster:

Linking Creativity to Problem-Solving:

Understand the inherent link between creativity and productivity. The Visionary planner recognizes that creative thinking is not just an artistic pursuit but a powerful problem-solving tool. Learn how engaging in creative activities within the planner enhances your ability to find innovative solutions to challenges.

Fueling Ideation and Innovation:

Explore how abundant space fuels ideation and innovation. The Visionary planner serves as a playground for brainstorming sessions, idea generation, and conceptualization. Whether you're envisioning a new project, business venture, or personal development plan, the planner becomes a catalyst for turning abstract concepts into tangible plans.

Integration with Goal Visualization:

Visual Representation of Ideas:

Discover how the Visionary planner allows for visual representation of your creative ideas. From mind maps that connect different concepts to visual timelines that showcase project progress, the planner becomes a visual aid that enhances your ability to comprehend and execute creative plans.

Alignment with Long-Term Goals:

Understand how creativity within the Visionary planner aligns with long-term goals. Creative spaces are not isolated; they contribute to the broader vision. Whether you're sketching a product design, drafting a business strategy, or visualizing personal growth, the planner ensures that your creative endeavors are connected to your overarching aspirations.

Realizing the Transformative Power:

Transformative Impact on Planning Experience:

Explore the transformative impact of fostering creativity within the Visionary planner. The planner becomes more than a tool for organizing tasks; it evolves into a dynamic space that reflects your individuality, embraces your creativity, and transforms the planning experience into a journey of self-expression.

Bringing Dreams to Life:

Understand the profound connection between creativity and bringing dreams to life. The Visionary planner, with its abundant space, becomes a vessel for turning imaginative ideas into tangible plans. Whether you're an artist, entrepreneur, or dreamer, the planner becomes a companion on the exciting journey of making your dreams a reality.

Fostering creativity with abundant space in the Visionary planner transcends the conventional boundaries of planning. It's an invitation to explore, imagine, and innovate, turning your planning experience into a dynamic and personal expression of your creative potential.

Chapter 5: Wellness and Mindfulness

- Wellness Warrior: Tracking health and wellness
- Encouraging healthy habits
- Mindful Maven: Living mindfully
- Mindfulness exercises and self-care

Wellness Warrior: Tracking Health and Wellness

Embark on a journey towards a healthier version of yourself as we explore the Wellness Warrior section of the planner. In this detailed guide, you'll discover how the Visionary planner transforms into your health companion, enabling you to track, monitor, and enhance your overall well-being.

Understanding the Wellness Warrior Section:

Holistic Approach to Well-being:

Dive into the holistic approach of the Wellness Warrior section. Unlike generic health trackers, this specialized part of the Visionary planner goes beyond mere data collection. It emphasizes a comprehensive view of well-being, encompassing physical, mental, and emotional aspects.

Purpose of Health Tracking:

Explore the purpose behind tracking health and wellness within the planner. The Wellness Warrior section is designed not only to record your activities but also to foster self-awareness. Understand how tracking becomes a tool for recognizing patterns, making informed choices, and cultivating a mindful approach to health.

Effective Strategies for Health Tracking:

Logging Meals and Workouts:

Learn how the Wellness Warrior section facilitates the logging of meals and workouts. It goes beyond calorie counting; it encourages you to document the nutritional content of your meals and the specifics of your workout routines. Understand the impact of this detailed tracking on making informed decisions about your health.

Monitoring Sleep Patterns:

Discover the significance of monitoring sleep patterns within the Wellness Warrior section. Quality sleep is a cornerstone of well-being, and the planner helps you establish connections between your sleep habits and overall health. Learn how this awareness contributes to creating a balanced and rejuvenating lifestyle.

Encouraging Healthy Habits:

Cultivating Positive Habits:

Explore how the Wellness Warrior section serves as a guide for cultivating positive habits. It goes beyond tracking to provide insights into building routines that support your well-being. Understand the role of consistency and gradual habit formation in fostering lasting and positive changes.

Setting and Achieving Health Goals:

Understand the goal-setting aspect of the Wellness Warrior section. It encourages you to set realistic health goals, whether related to fitness, nutrition, or stress management. Learn how the planner becomes a motivational tool, helping you take incremental steps towards achieving these goals.

Utilizing Monthly Reviews:

Reflecting on Progress:

Discover the importance of monthly reviews in the Wellness Warrior section. These reviews provide a structured space for reflecting on your health journey. Understand how reviewing your progress fosters a sense of achievement and motivation to continue making positive choices.

Adjusting Strategies:

Learn how monthly reviews allow for the adjustment of strategies. The Wellness Warrior section recognizes that well-being is a dynamic process, and your approach may need refinement. Understand how these reviews empower you to adapt and optimize your health and wellness strategies.

In the Wellness Warrior section, the Visionary planner becomes a trusted ally in your pursuit of a healthier lifestyle. From detailed tracking to cultivating positive habits and setting achievable goals, this section ensures that your well-being is not just a goal but a continuous and mindful journey.

Encouraging Healthy Habits

Embark on a transformative journey towards cultivating and maintaining healthy habits with the Visionary planner's Wellness Warrior section. In this comprehensive exploration, discover the strategies and approaches that make this section a powerful tool for achieving and sustaining a healthy lifestyle.

Understanding the Significance of Healthy Habits:

Holistic View of Health:

Delve into the holistic perspective that underlies the Wellness Warrior section. It doesn't just focus on isolated aspects of health but encourages a comprehensive view. Learn how cultivating healthy habits contributes not only to physical well-being but also to mental and emotional wellness.

Long-Term Impact:

Explore the long-term impact of cultivating healthy habits. The Wellness Warrior section emphasizes that the goal is not merely short-term changes but the establishment of sustainable practices. Understand how the integration of healthy habits into your daily routine contributes to a lasting and positive transformation.

Strategies for Cultivating Healthy Habits:

Personalized Habit Recommendations:

Discover how the Wellness Warrior section tailors its approach to your unique needs. It goes beyond generic advice, providing personalized habit recommendations based on your health goals. Learn how this individualized guidance enhances the effectiveness of habit cultivation.

Visualizing Progress:

Explore the visual tools within the Wellness Warrior section that aid in tracking and visualizing your progress. Visual representations of your journey, such as habit trackers and progress logs, provide a tangible way to see how your efforts are translating into positive outcomes. Understand the motivational power of visualizing your achievements.

Cultivating Positive Mindset:

Positive Reinforcement Techniques:

Understand how the Wellness Warrior section incorporates positive reinforcement techniques. It recognizes the psychological aspect of habit formation and employs affirmations, motivational quotes, and milestone celebrations to reinforce a positive mindset. Learn how these strategies contribute to a more optimistic and motivated approach to building healthy habits.

Mindful Awareness Practices:

Explore how mindfulness is integrated into the cultivation of healthy habits. The Wellness Warrior section introduces mindful awareness practices that encourage you to be present during your health-related activities. From mindful eating to conscious movement, discover how mindfulness enhances the overall effectiveness of habit-building.

Integration with Daily Routine:

Seamless Integration into Daily Life:

Discover how the Wellness Warrior section seamlessly integrates into your daily routine. It's not an additional task but becomes an intrinsic part of your daily activities. Learn how this integration ensures that cultivating healthy habits doesn't feel like a chore but becomes a natural and sustainable aspect of your lifestyle.

Aligned with Overall Well-being Goals:

Understand how the cultivation of healthy habits aligns with your broader well-being goals. The Wellness Warrior section ensures that the habits you develop contribute to achieving overarching health objectives. Explore the synergy between daily habits and long-term wellness within the planner.

Encouraging healthy habits with the Wellness Warrior section is not about adopting a short-lived fitness craze but about embracing a holistic and sustainable approach to well-being. From personalized recommendations to positive reinforcement and mindfulness integration, this section of the Visionary planner becomes your steadfast companion on the path to a healthier and happier you.

Living Mindfully with the Mindful Maven Section

Immerse yourself in the art of mindful living as we explore the Mindful Maven section within the Visionary planner. In this detailed guide, discover how this specialized section becomes your companion in cultivating mindfulness, fostering a serene and present-centered approach to daily life.

Understanding the Essence of Mindful Living:

Definition of Mindfulness:

Embark on the journey of understanding mindfulness within the Mindful Maven section. It goes beyond a mere concept and introduces mindfulness as a state of intentional, non-judgmental awareness of the present moment. Delve into the significance of cultivating this state for overall well-being.

Mindfulness as a Lifestyle:

Explore how the Mindful Maven section approaches mindfulness not as a practice confined to specific moments but as a lifestyle. Understand the integration of mindfulness into various aspects of daily life, from routine activities to significant events, fostering a continuous and pervasive sense of presence.

Incorporating Mindfulness into Daily Life:

Mindful Daily Activities:

Discover how the Mindful Maven section encourages the infusion of mindfulness into daily activities. From routine chores to work-related tasks, the planner provides guidance on incorporating mindful awareness. Learn how simple adjustments in your approach to daily activities contribute to a more mindful way of living.

Mindful Eating Practices:

Explore the role of mindfulness in eating habits. The Mindful Maven section introduces mindful eating practices, emphasizing the importance of savoring each bite, being attuned to hunger and fullness cues, and fostering a conscious relationship with food. Understand how mindful eating contributes to both physical and mental well-being.

Cultivating a Mindful Mindset:

Present-Centered Thinking:

Delve into the present-centered thinking promoted by the Mindful Maven section. It guides you in redirecting your focus to the current moment, releasing attachment to past concerns or future anxieties. Learn how this shift in mindset enhances clarity, reduces stress, and promotes a more tranquil mental state.

Mindful Stress Reduction Techniques:

Understand how mindfulness serves as a powerful tool for stress reduction. The Mindful Maven section introduces practical techniques for managing stress through mindfulness, including deep breathing exercises, meditation, and mindful movement. Explore how incorporating these practices into your routine fosters emotional resilience.

Integrating Mindfulness into Self-Care:

Self-Care as Mindful Practice:

Discover how the Mindful Maven section redefines self-care as a mindful practice. It goes beyond external treatments to emphasize internal well-being. Learn how mindfulness becomes an integral part of self-care routines, promoting a deeper connection with oneself and fostering a sense of inner peace.

Balancing Technology and Mindfulness:

Explore the delicate balance between technology use and mindfulness. The Mindful Maven section addresses the challenges of a digital age and provides insights into maintaining a mindful approach to technology. Learn how intentional use of digital devices can coexist with a mindful lifestyle.

Living mindfully with the Mindful Maven section is an exploration of the present moment, a journey towards tranquility in the midst of life's demands. From infusing mindfulness into daily activities to cultivating a mindful mindset and integrating it into self-care, this section of the Visionary planner becomes your guide in fostering a life marked by awareness, peace, and contentment.

Chapter 6: Superheroes of Planning

- Time Titan: Time blocking for efficiency
- Taskmaster: Prioritizing tasks effectively
- Efficiency Expert: Boosting overall productivity
- Real-life efficiency success stories

Time Titan: Time Blocking for Efficiency

Discover the superheroic powers of efficient time management with the Time Titan section of the Visionary planner. This section is not just a planner; it's your guide to becoming a master of time through the transformative technique of time blocking.

Understanding Time Blocking:

In the world of productivity, time blocking is the superhero cape you wear to conquer your daily tasks and goals. Let's break down the essence:

Definition and Concept:

Time blocking is your ally in the battle against scattered attention and unproductive multitasking. Embrace the idea of breaking your day into specific blocks, each dedicated to a particular task or type of activity. Imagine it as creating time zones for your work, allowing you to focus on one mission at a time.

Benefits of Time Blocking:

Uncover the superpowers bestowed upon you by time blocking. From heightened focus to increased task completion, this technique empowers you to make the most of every moment. Picture the satisfaction of seeing your to-do list shrink as you efficiently move through your dedicated time blocks.

Implementing Time Blocking Techniques:

Navigate the challenges of daily life with strategies tailored to make time blocking work for you:

Setting Priorities:

In the Time Titan section, learn the art of setting priorities. Gain insights into identifying tasks aligned with your overarching goals and allocating dedicated time blocks to them. This superheroic skill helps you distinguish between urgent and important tasks, ensuring your time is invested where it matters most.

Creating a Time-Blocked Schedule:

Craft a personalized time-blocked schedule using the Time Titan's customizable templates and guidelines. Learn how to structure your day effectively, allocating time for work, breaks, and personal activities. This superheroic schedule fosters a well-balanced routine that maximizes productivity without sacrificing your well-being.

Mastering Time Management Skills:

Enhance your time management prowess with advanced techniques:

Time Titan Techniques:

Explore advanced strategies within the Time Titan section. From the Pomodoro Technique's focused bursts to the Two-Minute Rule's efficiency, discover how these techniques complement time blocking. Adapt them to your unique working style and witness an extraordinary boost in productivity.

Adapting to Changing Priorities:

In a world of constant change, the Time Titan equips you to adapt seamlessly. Discover how the planner's tools and methods allow you to adjust time blocks when unexpected tasks arise. Learn to maintain productivity amid shifting priorities, embodying the resilience of a true time management superhero.

Real-Life Time Titan Success Stories:

Marvel at the inspiring tales of individuals who have embraced the Time Titan way:

Case Studies and Examples:

Dive into real-life success stories that showcase the transformative impact of time blocking. Explore how professionals, entrepreneurs, and creatives have harnessed the power of focused time management to achieve remarkable results. These case studies provide tangible proof of the Time Titan's effectiveness.

Tips for Overcoming Challenges:

Confront common challenges associated with time blocking and emerge victorious with practical tips. Whether battling procrastination or managing interruptions, the Time Titan section offers valuable insights. Learn to create an environment conducive to time-blocking success, ensuring that you overcome obstacles like a true superhero.

Equip yourself with the Time Titan section and embrace the superhero within, conquering time and achieving unparalleled efficiency in your daily life. Unleash the power of time blocking and witness your productivity soar to new heights.

Taskmaster: Prioritizing Tasks Effectively

Enter the realm of efficient task management with the Taskmaster section of the Visionary planner. In this segment, we unveil the superheroic abilities that enable you to become the master of prioritization, ensuring that your efforts align with what truly matters.

Understanding Prioritization Mastery:

Definition and Concept:

Taskmaster, the prioritization superhero, introduces you to the art of discerning what's urgent and important. Prioritization is the key to effective task management, allowing you to allocate your time and energy where it will yield the most significant impact. Imagine it as donning a task-focused lens that guides your daily decisions.

Benefits of Prioritization Mastery:

Unlock the extraordinary benefits bestowed upon you by mastering the art of prioritization. From increased productivity to a sense of accomplishment, Taskmaster empowers you to navigate your workload with precision. Visualize the satisfaction of tackling tasks in a strategic order, leading to consistent progress.

Implementing Effective Prioritization Techniques:

Navigate the sea of tasks with strategies designed for real-world success:

Eisenhower Matrix:

Discover the power of the Eisenhower Matrix, a prioritization tool that helps you categorize tasks based on urgency and importance. Taskmaster introduces you to this superheroic technique, guiding you to distinguish between tasks that demand immediate attention and those that contribute to long-term goals.

Task Priority Guidelines:

Learn practical guidelines within the Taskmaster section for setting task priorities. Understand how to assess the impact and urgency of each task, ensuring that your to-do list reflects your overarching objectives.

Taskmaster provides clarity on making informed decisions about where to direct your efforts.

Mastering the Art of Task Prioritization:

Taskmaster Techniques:

Explore advanced techniques offered by Taskmaster to elevate your task prioritization skills. From the ABCD method to the 1-3-5 Rule, understand how these strategies complement your prioritization efforts. Taskmaster equips you with a diverse toolkit, allowing you to tailor your approach to different scenarios.

Adapting to Changing Priorities:

Taskmaster ensures you are prepared for the unexpected. In a dynamic environment, learn how to adapt your task priorities when unforeseen challenges arise. Taskmaster's adaptability ensures that you can recalibrate your focus without losing momentum, showcasing the superheroic ability to navigate changing priorities seamlessly.

Real-Life Taskmaster Success Stories:

Case Studies and Examples:

Immerse yourself in real-life success stories of individuals who have harnessed the Taskmaster's prioritization powers. Explore scenarios where effective task prioritization has led to increased efficiency and goal attainment. These stories serve as practical illustrations of Taskmaster's impact on real-world productivity.

Tips for Overcoming Prioritization Challenges:

Taskmaster equips you with valuable tips for overcoming common challenges associated with task prioritization. Whether faced with conflicting deadlines or a high volume of tasks, discover how Taskmaster's principles guide you in making strategic decisions. Uncover the superheroic secrets to maintaining focus and order.

As you embrace the Taskmaster section, you step into a world where prioritization becomes second nature. The ability to discern and prioritize tasks effectively transforms you into a true task management superhero, ensuring that your efforts are aligned with your goals and objectives.

Efficiency Expert: Boosting Overall Productivity

Embark on a transformative journey toward peak productivity with the Efficiency Expert section of the Visionary planner. In this section, we delve deep into the superheroic strategies designed to enhance your efficiency across every facet of your life.

Understanding Productivity Enhancement:

Definition and Concept:

Efficiency Expert, your productivity ally, introduces you to the intricacies of streamlining your tasks and optimizing your workflows. At its essence, productivity enhancement is about achieving more in less time while maintaining a high standard of output. Visualize Efficiency Expert as your guide to working smarter, employing strategies that bring about tangible results and elevate your overall efficiency.

Benefits of Productivity Enhancement:

Uncover the remarkable benefits that come with boosting overall productivity. Efficiency Expert empowers you to navigate your daily tasks with precision, leading to a sense of accomplishment, reduced stress, and increased satisfaction. Picture the satisfaction of achieving your goals effortlessly, thanks to a systematic approach to productivity.

Implementing Efficiency Enhancement Techniques:

Dive into the actionable strategies that define the Efficiency Expert:

Time-Saving Techniques:

Efficiency Expert equips you with a repertoire of time-saving techniques designed to optimize your daily routines. Explore the power of batch processing, where similar tasks are grouped and tackled consecutively, minimizing the mental energy required to switch between activities. Additionally, embrace the simplicity of the two-minute rule, swiftly completing tasks that take two minutes or less. Efficiency Expert ensures that these techniques seamlessly integrate into your lifestyle, making productivity a natural part of your routine.

Time-Saving Techniques Unveiled by the Efficiency Expert:

In your pursuit of peak productivity, Efficiency Expert introduces an arsenal of time-saving techniques, each carefully crafted to optimize your daily routines. Let's explore these techniques, understanding why they are efficient, how to implement them seamlessly into your lifestyle, and when to apply them for maximum impact.

1. Batch Processing:

Why it's Efficient:

Batch processing is a powerhouse technique that capitalizes on the principle of minimizing task-switching. When you group similar tasks and tackle them consecutively, you reduce the mental overhead associated with switching between different activities. The brain is exceptionally adept at maintaining focus when engaged in a specific type of task, making batch processing a highly efficient strategy.

How to Implement:

Identify tasks that share commonalities, whether in theme, skill set, or required resources. Group these tasks together and designate specific time blocks for their execution. For instance, if your work involves responding to emails, writing reports, or conducting research, allocate dedicated time slots for each category rather than scattering them throughout the day.

When to Apply:

Batch processing is particularly effective for tasks that require similar mental resources or involve using the same tools. Apply this technique to activities such as responding to emails, making phone calls, or completing creative tasks. By doing so, you minimize cognitive load, enhance focus, and optimize your efficiency.

2. The Two-Minute Rule:

Why it's Efficient:

The Two-Minute Rule is rooted in the idea that small tasks, when addressed immediately, prevent them from accumulating and becoming overwhelming. Swiftly completing tasks that take two minutes or less eliminates procrastination and ensures that minor responsibilities don't linger, freeing up mental space for more substantial endeavors.

How to Implement:

As you encounter tasks that are quick to complete, assess whether they fall within the two-minute timeframe. If so, tackle them immediately. This could include responding to short emails, organizing your workspace, or scheduling brief appointments. The key is to address these tasks promptly, preventing them from accumulating on your to-do list.

When to Apply:

Apply the Two-Minute Rule to tasks that are simple, quick, and do not require extensive planning or execution. By incorporating this rule into your routine, you create a habit of immediate action, maintaining a sense of control over your workload. It's particularly effective for preventing minor tasks from snowballing into larger, more time-consuming projects.

Efficiency Expert ensures that these time-saving techniques seamlessly integrate into your daily life, becoming ingrained habits rather than isolated strategies. As you adopt batch processing and the Two-Minute Rule, you cultivate a proactive approach to task management, optimizing your efficiency and reclaiming valuable time for more impactful endeavors. Remember, the key lies in consistent application and adaptation to your unique workflow, making these techniques powerful allies on your journey to productivity mastery.

Task Optimization Guidelines:

Within the Efficiency Expert section, discover practical guidelines for optimizing tasks and workflows. Learn to evaluate the efficiency of your current processes, identifying areas where improvements can be made. Efficiency Expert provides you with a systematic approach to task optimization, helping you streamline your efforts for maximum impact. From setting clear objectives to breaking tasks into manageable steps, these guidelines empower you to enhance your productivity systematically.

Task Optimization Guidelines Unveiled by the Efficiency Expert:

In the Efficiency Expert section, you're not just introduced to the concept of task optimization; you're handed a toolkit of practical guidelines that empower you to systematically enhance your productivity. Let's dive into these guidelines, understanding what they entail, how to implement them into your daily routine, and when to apply each for maximum impact.

1. Evaluate and Assess Current Processes:

What it Entails:

Efficiency Expert encourages you to embark on a journey of self-reflection and assessment. Take a close look at your current processes and workflows. Identify tasks that consume significant time and energy, and evaluate whether there are redundancies or areas for improvement. This step is foundational to understanding where optimization efforts should be concentrated.

How to Implement:

Create a list of your regular tasks and processes. For each, assess the time invested, the resources utilized, and the outcomes achieved. Look for patterns, bottlenecks, or activities that might be hindering efficiency. Efficiency Expert provides templates or frameworks for this evaluation, ensuring a structured and comprehensive assessment.

When to Apply:

Regularly conduct these evaluations to stay proactive in identifying opportunities for improvement. This could be on a weekly or monthly basis, depending on the nature of your work. Use this guideline whenever you sense a shift in your workload or whenever you're seeking continuous improvement in your processes.

2. Systematic Approach to Task Optimization:

What it Entails:

Efficiency Expert introduces a systematic approach to task optimization. Rather than approaching optimization sporadically, this guideline advocates for a structured methodology. This involves categorizing tasks based on urgency, importance, or complexity and applying tailored optimization strategies to each category.

How to Implement:

Organize your tasks into categories, considering factors such as deadlines, priority, and complexity. For urgent tasks, focus on time-saving techniques like batch processing. For complex tasks, break them down into manageable steps. The Efficiency Expert section provides a step-by-step guide to this categorization and optimization process.

Apply this guideline whenever you're faced with a diverse set of tasks that require varying levels of attention. By adopting a systematic approach, you ensure that your optimization efforts are targeted and tailored to the specific demands of each task.

3. Setting Clear Objectives:

What it Entails:

Efficiency Expert emphasizes the importance of setting clear objectives before diving into any task. Define the purpose, desired outcomes, and key milestones for each activity. This guideline ensures that your efforts are aligned with overarching goals, preventing wasted time on activities that don't contribute to your objectives.

How to Implement:

Before commencing any task, take a moment to articulate clear objectives. Ask yourself what you aim to achieve, why it's important, and how success will be measured. Efficiency Expert provides prompts or templates for objective-setting to make this process intuitive and effective.

When to Apply:

Apply this guideline at the beginning of each work session or when taking on a new project. It ensures that your efforts are purposeful and aligned with your broader goals, preventing aimless work and enhancing overall efficiency.

4. Breaking Tasks into Manageable Steps:

What it Entails:

Efficiency Expert guides you to break down larger tasks into smaller, more manageable steps. This guideline acknowledges that complex tasks can be overwhelming when approached as a whole. Breaking them into smaller components not only makes them more achievable but also facilitates better planning and execution.

How to Implement:

Identify tasks that seem daunting in their entirety. Efficiently divide them into smaller, actionable steps. For example, if you're tasked with writing a report, break it down into outlining, drafting, reviewing, and finalizing. Efficiency Expert provides frameworks or methodologies to simplify this process.

When to Apply:

Apply this guideline whenever faced with a task that appears intricate or time-consuming. Breaking tasks into manageable steps makes the overall process more digestible, allowing you to maintain focus and progress steadily.

Examples of Task Optimization in Action:

Example 1: Email Management

Let's say you evaluate your email management process and discover that responding to emails throughout the day is hindering your focus. Applying the systematic approach, you categorize emails based on urgency and importance. You decide to batch process emails twice a day, allocating specific time slots. This optimizes your email management process, freeing up uninterrupted blocks for more concentrated work.

Example 2: Project Planning

When faced with a complex project, Efficiency Expert suggests setting clear objectives and breaking down the project into manageable steps. You define the project's purpose, outline key milestones, and then systematically break it into phases. This approach ensures that your efforts are aligned with project goals and that each step contributes to the overall success of the project.

By implementing these task optimization guidelines from the Efficiency Expert, you transform your approach to work. Each guideline provides a practical, actionable framework that seamlessly integrates into your routine, ensuring that your productivity efforts are not only intentional but consistently refined for maximum impact.

Mastering the Art of Productivity Enhancement:

Unleash the advanced techniques that elevate you to new heights of productivity:

Efficiency Expert Techniques:

Explore sophisticated techniques within the Efficiency Expert section, designed to cater to your unique needs and goals. Dive into the world of automation tools that handle repetitive tasks, freeing up your time for more complex endeavors. Delve into delegation strategies, understanding how to distribute tasks effectively among team members or collaborators. Efficiency Expert provides you with a diverse set of tools, each tailored to amplify your efficiency in specific contexts.

Efficiency Expert Techniques Unveiled: Elevating Your Productivity Game

Within the Efficiency Expert section, you're not just presented with abstract concepts; you're handed a toolkit of sophisticated techniques tailored to cater to your unique needs and goals. Let's delve into this world of efficiency enhancement, exploring the tools at your disposal, understanding how to seamlessly implement them, and identifying the ideal contexts for their application.

1. Automation Tools:

What They Are:

Automation tools are your digital assistants, designed to handle repetitive and time-consuming tasks with precision and efficiency. These tools range from email automation platforms to project management software that can streamline your workflows, allowing you to focus on tasks that require your unique skills and decision-making.

How to Implement:

Identify tasks in your daily routine that are repetitive and rule-based. These could include sending routine emails, updating spreadsheets, or managing calendar events. Efficiency Expert guides you in selecting the right automation tools for these tasks. For instance, tools like Zapier or Microsoft Power Automate can automate data transfers between your apps, saving you valuable time and reducing the risk of errors.

When to Apply:

Apply automation tools when faced with repetitive tasks that consume a significant portion of your time. This could be daily data entry, social media posting schedules, or email responses. By automating these processes, you ensure consistency and accuracy, liberating your time for more strategic and creative endeavors.

2. Delegation Strategies:

What They Are:

Delegation strategies involve distributing tasks effectively among team members or collaborators. This is a powerful technique for leveraging the strengths of individuals within your professional network, ensuring that each task is assigned to the most suitable person based on their skills and expertise.

How to Implement:

Efficiency Expert equips you with strategies to assess team members' strengths and allocate tasks accordingly. For example, if you have a team member with strong analytical skills, delegate data analysis tasks to them. Use project management tools like Asana or Trello to assign and track tasks, fostering clear communication and accountability.

When to Apply:

Apply delegation strategies when facing a workload that exceeds your capacity or when specific tasks require specialized skills. It's especially effective for collaborative projects where the diverse expertise of team members can be harnessed. Efficiency Expert helps you identify tasks suitable for delegation and provides guidance on fostering a collaborative work environment.

3. Calendar Optimization Techniques:

What They Are:

Calendar optimization techniques involve maximizing the use of your calendar to enhance productivity. This includes time-blocking strategies, setting realistic deadlines, and integrating your calendar with other productivity tools to create a comprehensive schedule.

How to Implement:

Efficiency Expert introduces you to advanced calendar features and techniques. For instance, using time-blocking, you allocate specific time slots for different types of tasks, ensuring a structured and focused workday. Integrating your calendar with task management tools like Todoist or Notion enables a seamless transition from planning to execution.

When to Apply:

Apply calendar optimization techniques when seeking better time management, reducing procrastination, and ensuring that your schedule aligns with your priorities. This is particularly effective for individuals juggling multiple roles or projects. Efficiency Expert provides insights into creating a personalized calendar strategy based on your unique workflow.

Examples of Technique Application:

Example 1: Automation in Email Responses

Efficiency Expert suggests using email automation tools like Boomerang or Mailchimp for routine email responses. By creating templates or automated sequences, you save time spent on repetitive replies, ensuring that your inbox remains organized and responses are consistent.

Example 2: Delegating Project Tasks

When faced with a complex project, Efficiency Expert recommends using delegation strategies. Identify tasks aligning with team members' strengths and delegate accordingly. Tools like Slack or Microsoft Teams facilitate seamless communication, ensuring that everyone is on the same page.

Example 3: Time-Blocking for Daily Planning

Efficiency Expert encourages the use of time-blocking for daily planning. Allocate specific time slots for focused work, meetings, and breaks. Calendar integration with task management tools helps create a holistic schedule that balances productivity and well-being.

By exploring these Efficiency Expert techniques, you not only optimize your efficiency but also gain valuable insights into tailoring these strategies to fit your unique circumstances. The goal is not just to improve productivity but to cultivate a sustainable and adaptable approach to managing your time and tasks.

Adapting to Changing Workflows:

Efficiency Expert ensures you are not just efficient but adaptable. In a dynamic work environment, learn to adjust your efficiency strategies in response to new challenges or opportunities. Efficiency Expert's adaptability ensures that you stay ahead of the curve, effortlessly navigating changes in your workflow. The superheroic ability to adapt ensures that your efficiency remains unwavering in the face of evolving circumstances.

Real-Life Efficiency Expert Success Stories:

Immerse yourself in the real-life success stories of individuals who have harnessed the strategies of the Efficiency Expert. These stories provide tangible examples of how enhanced productivity has translated into significant achievements and personal satisfaction. Whether it's professionals achieving ambitious career goals or individuals finding a harmonious work-life balance, Efficiency Expert's principles have transformative effects.

Tips for Overcoming Productivity Challenges:

Efficiency Expert equips you with invaluable tips for overcoming common challenges associated with productivity. Whether you're managing multiple responsibilities or juggling competing priorities, Efficiency Expert's principles provide actionable insights. Learn the superheroic secrets to staying focused, effective, and resilient in the face of productivity challenges.

As you fully embrace the Efficiency Expert section, you step into a realm where productivity is not just a goal; it's a superpower. The ability to enhance efficiency across various aspects of your life transforms you into a true Efficiency Expert, ensuring that every action contributes to your overall success and fulfillment. Efficiency becomes your ally, propelling you toward your goals with unparalleled precision and ease.

Unlocking Efficiency: Real-Life Success Stories

In the final section of Chapter 6, we dive into the tangible impact of the productivity superheroes introduced earlier—Time Titan, Taskmaster, and Efficiency Expert. These real-life efficiency success stories illustrate how individuals and organizations have transformed their productivity using these strategies. Let's explore these narratives to understand the practical application of these superhero techniques.

Time Titan Triumphs:
Case Study: The Pomodoro Technique

Sarah, a freelance writer, struggled with procrastination and distractions. With the guidance of Time Titan's time-blocking principles, she embraced the Pomodoro Technique. Breaking her work into focused 25-minute intervals (Pomodoros) followed by short breaks, Sarah witnessed a significant boost in her writing output. The structured time blocks enhanced her concentration, and the short breaks kept her refreshed. This Time Titan strategy not only improved Sarah's efficiency but also contributed to her overall well-being.

Taskmaster's Impact:
Case Study: Project Prioritization in a Marketing Team

Mark, a marketing manager, faced the challenge of a demanding workload and competing priorities. Taskmaster's approach to prioritizing tasks effectively came to his rescue. Using techniques like the Eisenhower Matrix, Mark classified tasks based on urgency and importance. This allowed his team to focus on high-priority tasks, leading to increased project efficiency. Taskmaster's emphasis on strategic task prioritization proved instrumental in achieving the marketing team's objectives.

Efficiency Expert in Action:
Case Study: Streamlining Administrative Tasks

Emma, a small business owner, grappled with administrative tasks consuming much of her time. Efficiency Expert's time-saving techniques, including automation tools like Zapier, transformed her workflow. By automating invoice generation, email responses, and data entry, Emma reclaimed valuable hours. The Efficiency Expert approach not only increased efficiency but also empowered Emma to redirect her energy towards business growth and client relationships.

Real-life Efficiency Champions:
Case Study: Collaborative Project Management

Alex and Jessica, co-founders of a tech startup, embodied the synergy of Time Titan, Taskmaster, and Efficiency Expert. Implementing collaborative project management tools like Asana, they streamlined communication, task delegation, and progress tracking. The real-life efficiency success of their startup exemplifies how these superheroes, when combined, create a robust framework for organizational productivity.

Key Takeaways from Success Stories:

- Adaptability: These success stories highlight the adaptability of the presented techniques. Each individual tailored the strategies to fit their unique circumstances and challenges.
- Measurable Impact: Time Titan, Taskmaster, and Efficiency Expert aren't just theoretical concepts—they produce tangible results. The success stories demonstrate how applying these techniques can lead to increased output, better time management, and enhanced overall productivity.
- Holistic Approach: Combining strategies from all three superheroes often yields the most significant results. Real-life examples emphasize the synergy between time blocking, task prioritization, and efficiency tools for a holistic and sustainable approach to productivity.

By exploring these real-life efficiency success stories, you gain insights into the transformative power of the techniques presented in this chapter. The superheroes of planning aren't mythical; they're accessible tools that, when wielded effectively, can turn productivity aspirations into reality.

Chapter 7: Holistic Approaches

- Balance Builder: Achieving work-life equilibrium
- Reflection Rookie: Personal growth and reflection
- Self-reflection, goal setting, progress tracking
- Real-life stories of balance and growth

Chapter 7: Holistic Approaches to Work and Life Harmony

Chapter 7 explores holistic approaches that extend beyond conventional productivity tools, concentrating on the attainment of work-life equilibrium and personal growth through self-reflection. Let's delve into the intricacies of the first section:

Balance Builder: Achieving Work-Life Equilibrium

Balance Builder introduces a transformative perspective on time management by highlighting the significance of striking a harmonious balance between professional commitments and personal well-being. This section unfolds practical strategies, real-world examples, and narratives that guide individuals toward a more balanced and fulfilling lifestyle.

Understanding Work-Life Equilibrium:

Work-life equilibrium isn't a perfect time split; it's about ensuring neither work nor personal life dominates the other. Balance Builder introduces the concept of "boundary management," encouraging individuals to set clear limits to prevent work encroaching on personal time and vice versa.

Example:

Jane, a marketing executive, battled burnout due to extended work hours. Through Balance Builder, she learned to set boundaries, designating specific times for work and personal activities. This not only boosted her job satisfaction but also enhanced her overall life contentment.

Strategies for Work-Life Equilibrium:

Balance Builder provides actionable strategies, including effective time management, setting realistic expectations, and fostering open communication. The section explores the "time-blocking" technique, urging individuals to allocate dedicated time for work, personal activities, and leisure.

Example:

Mark, a project manager, adopted time-blocking to ensure focused work hours and designated family time. This not only improved his project management skills but also strengthened his relationships at home.

Recognizing Signs of Imbalance:

Identifying signs of imbalance is crucial. Balance Builder equips individuals with awareness to recognize stress indicators, burnout symptoms, and strained relationships. By understanding these signs, individuals can proactively address issues and recalibrate their priorities.

Example:

Sarah, a software developer, understood the importance of recognizing signs of imbalance when she noticed a decline in her overall well-being. Through Balance Builder, she learned to identify stress triggers and take preventive measures, ensuring a healthier work-life dynamic.

Case Studies of Work-Life Equilibrium:

The section concludes with real-life case studies illustrating successful implementation of Balance Builder strategies. These stories showcase individuals who have achieved a harmonious work-life balance, emphasizing that it's an attainable goal regardless of the nature of one's profession.

Example:

John, an entrepreneur, shares his journey of transforming a high-stress work environment into a balanced one. Through the strategies presented in Balance Builder, he not only improved his business performance but also enhanced his overall life satisfaction.

Key Takeaways:

- Harmony, Not Equality: Work-life equilibrium is about creating harmony, acknowledging that certain periods may require more focus on work, while others may demand attention to personal matters.
- Proactive Boundary Management: Balance Builder emphasizes proactive boundary management, teaching individuals to set boundaries to protect their personal time, preventing burnout, and fostering sustained well-being.
- Tailoring Strategies: The strategies presented in this section are adaptable and can be tailored to individual preferences and circumstances. It encourages readers to experiment with different approaches to find what works best for them.

By exploring Balance Builder, readers gain insights into achieving a holistic work-life equilibrium, paving the way for increased satisfaction in both professional and personal realms.

Reflection Rookie: Personal Growth and Reflection

Reflection Rookie introduces a transformative perspective on personal development and growth through the power of self-reflection. This section provides actionable insights, practical examples, and real-world applications to guide individuals on a journey of continuous improvement.

Understanding Personal Growth:
Reflection Rookie lays the foundation by defining personal growth as an ongoing process of self-improvement, learning, and development. It emphasizes the idea that personal growth extends beyond professional achievements, encompassing aspects of emotional intelligence, resilience, and overall well-being.

Example:

> Emily, an aspiring professional, experienced significant personal growth by recognizing her strengths and weaknesses through reflective practices. This awareness empowered her to make informed decisions, fostering resilience in the face of challenges.

Importance of Self-Reflection:
This section delves into the significance of self-reflection as a tool for personal growth. It explains that self-reflection is the process of looking inward, examining one's thoughts, actions, and experiences. The emphasis is on fostering mindfulness and self-awareness to make intentional choices aligned with personal values.

Example:

> James, a young entrepreneur, found that regular self-reflection allowed him to identify patterns of behavior that hindered his growth. By addressing these patterns, he cultivated a more mindful and intentional approach to his personal and professional life.

Practical Techniques for Reflection:
Reflection Rookie provides practical techniques to incorporate self-reflection into daily life. It explores methods such as journaling, meditation, and goal-setting exercises. The aim is to empower readers to choose techniques that resonate with them, making reflection an accessible and personalized

practice.

Example:

> Sarah, a busy parent, integrated short mindfulness exercises into her daily routine. These brief moments of reflection allowed her to stay connected with her personal growth journey amid a hectic schedule.

Setting Personal Goals:
Personal growth often involves setting and pursuing meaningful goals. Reflection Rookie introduces the concept of SMART goals (Specific, Measurable, Achievable, Relevant, Time-bound) and guides readers in aligning their goals with their broader vision for personal development.

Example:

> David, a student, utilized SMART goals to enhance his study habits. By setting specific and achievable objectives, he witnessed tangible improvements in his academic performance and overall well-being.

Real-Life Stories of Reflection and Growth:
The section concludes with real-life stories illustrating the transformative power of self-reflection. These stories showcase individuals who, through consistent reflection, overcame challenges, discovered their true potential, and experienced substantial personal growth.

Example:

> Rachel, a career professional, shares her journey of navigating a career change through intentional reflection. By assessing her skills, values, and aspirations, she successfully transitioned to a more fulfilling and aligned career path.

Key Takeaways:

- Continuous Learning: Personal growth is a continuous learning journey that extends beyond professional achievements, focusing on emotional intelligence, resilience, and overall well-being.
- Mindful Self-Reflection: Emphasizes the importance of mindful self-reflection, allowing individuals to gain insights into their thoughts, actions, and experiences for intentional decision-making.

- Practical Integration: Provides practical techniques for integrating reflection into daily life, accommodating various preferences and schedules.
- SMART Goal Setting: Encourages the setting of SMART goals aligned with personal values, fostering intentional progress and development.
- Real-Life Inspirations: Real-life stories highlight the transformative power of reflection, showcasing individuals who achieved significant personal growth through mindful self-reflection.

By delving into Reflection Rookie, readers gain valuable insights and tools to embark on a personal growth journey, fostering a fulfilling and purpose-driven life.

Self-Reflection, Goal Setting, Progress Tracking

This section delves into the synergy of self-reflection, goal setting, and progress tracking, offering a comprehensive guide to align personal aspirations with tangible achievements. Let's unpack the details:

The Interplay of Self-Reflection and Goal Setting:
This section emphasizes how self-reflection serves as the compass for effective goal setting. It introduces the concept of introspective questioning, encouraging individuals to assess their values, strengths, and areas for improvement before defining their goals.

In this crucial aspect of personal development, the synergy between self-reflection and goal setting becomes the cornerstone for achieving meaningful and purpose-driven aspirations.

Understanding Introspective Questioning:
Introspective questioning involves a deep dive into one's thoughts, feelings, and experiences. It prompts individuals to ask themselves profound questions about their desires, motivations, and the aspects of life that bring them fulfillment. Through this process, people gain clarity about their values, uncover strengths they may not have consciously recognized, and identify areas for improvement.

Example:
Before embarking on a career change, Sarah engaged in introspective questioning. She asked herself, "What aspects of my current job bring me joy? Where do I see myself making a meaningful impact?" These questions revealed her passion for community engagement and directed her toward setting career goals aligned with this newfound insight.

Aligning Aspirations with Values:
Self-reflection acts as a compass, guiding individuals to align their aspirations with their deeply held values. By evaluating personal beliefs, principles, and what truly matters to them, individuals can set goals that resonate with their core identity. This alignment enhances motivation and fosters a sense of purpose, as the goals become an extension of one's authentic self.

Example:
Mark, a budding entrepreneur, aligned his business goals with his values of sustainability and ethical practices. This alignment not only

provided him with a clear direction for his venture but also fueled a sense of fulfillment in contributing to causes he cared about.

Recognizing Strengths and Areas for Improvement:
The process of self-reflection encourages individuals to recognize their strengths and acknowledge areas where improvement is possible. Understanding one's strengths allows for leveraging them in goal pursuit, while recognizing areas for improvement opens avenues for personal growth and skill development.

Example:
Emily, an aspiring graphic designer, identified her strength in creativity during self-reflection. Simultaneously, she recognized the need to improve her project management skills. This insight guided her in setting goals that capitalized on her creativity while also addressing her developmental areas.

Setting Purposeful Goals:
Armed with a profound understanding of values, strengths, and areas for improvement, individuals can set purposeful and authentic goals. These goals are not mere benchmarks but become integral to a person's journey toward self-fulfillment. The process of goal setting, informed by self-reflection, ensures that the pursuit is aligned with one's identity and aspirations.

Example:
James, a fitness enthusiast, set a purposeful goal of running a marathon after reflecting on his love for outdoor activities and the sense of achievement he derived from physical challenges. This goal, rooted in self-awareness, motivated him through the rigorous training process.

Continuous Adaptation through Reflection:
Importantly, self-reflection doesn't end with goal setting—it remains a dynamic process throughout the journey. Individuals continuously adapt their goals based on evolving self-awareness and changing life circumstances. Regular reflection ensures that goals stay relevant and aligned with one's evolving values and aspirations.

Example:
Maria periodically revisited her career goals through ongoing self-reflection. As her interests evolved, she adapted her goals to stay aligned with her changing passions, ensuring that her career remained a source of fulfillment.

In essence, the interplay of self-reflection and goal setting is a transformative process. It empowers individuals to set goals that are not just externally defined markers but are deeply rooted in self-awareness, authenticity, and a genuine understanding of one's values and potential. Through this interplay, individuals embark on a purpose-driven journey toward personal and professional fulfillment.

Example:

> Maria, a young professional, utilized self-reflection to identify her passion for community engagement. This introspection guided her in setting meaningful goals aligned with her values, such as initiating a local volunteering project.

SMART Goal Setting Revisited:

Building on the earlier discussion of SMART goals, this part revisits the concept with a focus on personal development. It provides a step-by-step guide on crafting specific, measurable, achievable, relevant, and time-bound goals tailored to individual growth.

In the realm of personal development, the revisitation of SMART goals offers a strategic and deliberate approach to crafting objectives that are both meaningful and attainable. This section is designed to guide individuals through the process of setting goals that align with their personal growth journey.

Specific Goals:
Definition: Specific goals are clear, detailed, and unambiguous objectives that leave no room for interpretation.
Elaboration: When setting specific goals, individuals define the desired outcome with precision. For instance, instead of a vague goal like "improve fitness," a specific goal would be "complete a 5k run within the next three months."
Example:
Tom, aspiring to enhance his communication skills, set a specific goal: "Deliver a confident and engaging presentation at the company meeting next month."

Measurable Progress:
Definition: Measurable goals are quantifiable, allowing individuals to track progress and assess the degree of achievement.
Elaboration: Measuring progress involves incorporating tangible

metrics. For example, a measurable goal related to enhanced productivity might be "reduce response time to emails by 20% within the next two weeks."
Example:
Sarah aimed for improved time management, establishing a measurable goal: "Complete all daily tasks and assignments at least 30 minutes before the end of the workday."

Achievable Objectives:

Definition: Achievable goals are realistic and within the realm of possibility, considering resources, skills, and constraints.
Elaboration: While aiming high is commendable, achievable goals ensure that individuals set objectives that are challenging yet feasible. For instance, an achievable goal could be "complete an online coding course to learn a new programming language in the next three months."
Example:
Emily set an achievable goal for career growth: "Attain a professional certification relevant to my field within the next six months."

Relevance to Personal Growth:

Definition: Relevant goals align with an individual's values, aspirations, and overarching personal development journey.
Elaboration: Relevance ensures that the goals contribute meaningfully to one's growth. For example, a relevant goal for enhancing well-being might be "practice mindfulness meditation for 10 minutes daily to reduce stress and enhance focus."
Example:
Mark, prioritizing work-life balance, set a relevant goal: "Designate Sundays as family time and avoid work-related activities on that day."

Time-Bound Commitments:

Definition: Time-bound goals have a set timeframe, creating a sense of urgency and providing a deadline for achievement.
Elaboration: Incorporating a specific time frame adds a crucial dimension to goal setting. For instance, a time-bound goal for skill development could be "complete an online language course in the next eight weeks."
Example:
Jessica, aspiring for a healthier lifestyle, set a time-bound goal: "Achieve a consistent workout routine of at least three times a week for the next three months."

By revisiting SMART goal setting within the context of personal development, individuals gain a practical framework to transform their aspirations into tangible and achievable objectives. This approach empowers individuals to navigate their growth journey with clarity, focus, and a systematic plan for success.

Example:

> Jake, a recent graduate, applied the SMART criteria to his personal development goals. By breaking down broader aspirations into actionable steps, he witnessed a systematic and measurable progression in his skills and knowledge.

Progress Tracking for Motivation and Adaptation:

In the pursuit of personal growth, the significance of progress tracking cannot be overstated. This section unfolds the pivotal role that tracking plays as a powerful motivational tool and a dynamic strategy for adaptation. Let's delve into why tracking matters, explore diverse tracking methods, and understand how it contributes to sustained motivation and adaptive growth.

Importance of Progress Tracking:

Introduction: Progress tracking serves as a compass on your personal development journey, providing a tangible record of your achievements, milestones, and areas for improvement.

Elaboration: When you track your progress, you create a visual roadmap of your evolution, fostering a sense of accomplishment and motivation. It allows you to witness the tangible results of your efforts, reinforcing your commitment to continued growth.

Example:

Rachel, on her fitness journey, found immense motivation by tracking her weekly running distances. Witnessing the gradual increase in mileage became a source of pride and encouragement.

Various Tracking Methods:

Introduction: There are diverse methods to track progress, catering to different preferences and lifestyles.

Elaboration:

- Journaling Achievements:
  Description: Keeping a personal journal where you document your achievements, reflections, and setbacks.
  Example:

Alex maintained a journal to record his daily accomplishments, noting both professional achievements and personal victories.

- Technology-Based Tools:
  Description: Leveraging apps, spreadsheets, or specialized tools to digitally track progress and visualize data.
  Example:
  Sarah used a habit-tracking app to monitor her daily meditation practice, receiving reminders and insights into her consistency.
- Visual Progress Boards:
  Description: Creating a visual board or collage that represents your goals and progress.
  Example:
  Mike, aspiring to learn a new language, designed a visual board with images of landmarks from the target country, marking each milestone.

Emphasizing the Role of Tracking:
Introduction: Beyond mere documentation, tracking actively influences your mindset, helping you stay motivated and adapt your strategies.
Elaboration: Regularly reviewing your tracked data allows you to identify patterns, recognize areas for improvement, and celebrate milestones. It transforms your journey into an interactive process, encouraging proactive adjustments to optimize your growth trajectory.
Example:
Emily, in her career development, used quarterly reviews of her tracked accomplishments to refine her professional goals and focus on areas where additional skills were needed.

By understanding the importance of progress tracking, exploring diverse methods, and emphasizing its role in motivation and adaptation, individuals can harness this tool to propel their personal growth forward. Whether through the simplicity of journaling or the sophistication of technology-based solutions, tracking becomes a dynamic companion on the path to continuous improvement.

Example:

Emily, an aspiring writer, maintained a progress journal to track her daily writing goals. This not only celebrated small wins but also allowed her to adapt her writing routine based on what proved most effective.

Celebrating Milestones:
Acknowledging the significance of celebrating milestones, this part explores the psychological impact of recognizing achievements. It encourages readers to appreciate both small and significant milestones, fostering a positive mindset and reinforcing the journey of personal development.

Example:

David, a fitness enthusiast, celebrated each milestone in his fitness journey, whether it was running an extra mile or achieving a personal best in weightlifting. These celebrations became motivating markers in his ongoing progress.

Real-Life Stories of Personal Growth:
The section concludes with real-life stories showcasing individuals who effectively combined self-reflection, goal setting, and progress tracking. These narratives exemplify how this holistic approach led to transformative personal growth.

Example:

Sarah, a career professional, shares her story of combining introspective reflection, strategic goal setting, and diligent progress tracking to pivot her career toward her passion, demonstrating the power of a holistic approach.

Key Takeaways:

- Guided Goal Setting: Self-reflection guides effective goal setting by prompting individuals to align their aspirations with their values and strengths.
- SMART Goals for Personal Development: Revisiting SMART goals, this section illustrates how to apply the criteria specifically to personal development, ensuring clarity and measurability.
- Motivational Progress Tracking: Progress tracking serves as a motivational tool, enabling individuals to stay focused, adapt strategies, and celebrate incremental achievements.
- Importance of Celebration: Acknowledging and celebrating milestones fosters a positive mindset and reinforces the value of the personal development journey.
- Real-Life Inspirations: Real-life stories demonstrate the transformative impact of combining self-reflection, goal setting, and progress

tracking, inspiring readers to embark on their holistic personal growth journey.

By immersing in this section, readers gain practical insights into intertwining self-reflection, goal setting, and progress tracking, fostering a structured and meaningful path to personal development.

Real-Life Stories of Balance and Growth:

This concluding section of Chapter 7 brings the principles of balance and personal growth to life through real-world narratives. By delving into these stories, readers gain practical insights into how individuals successfully achieved equilibrium in their work and personal lives, fostering tangible growth. Let's explore the details of these real-life stories, highlighting the strategies employed, challenges overcome, and the broader lessons they offer.

Narrative 1: Work-Life Integration Mastery
Introduction: Meet Sarah, a marketing professional who seamlessly integrated her work and personal life, challenging the conventional notion of work-life balance.
Elaboration:
- Strategies Employed:
  Sarah embraced a flexible work schedule, leveraging remote work options and prioritizing tasks based on their impact. She blurred the lines between work and personal time, finding harmony in a holistic approach to her daily activities.
- Challenges Overcome:
  Juggling multiple responsibilities posed occasional challenges for Sarah. However, by establishing clear boundaries, maintaining open communication with her team, and cultivating a supportive work environment, she navigated these challenges with resilience.
- Lessons Learned:
  Sarah's story underscores the importance of adapting traditional concepts of balance to fit the demands of a dynamic work landscape. Her ability to integrate work and life seamlessly offers a valuable lesson in embracing flexibility and redefining balance on individual terms.

Narrative 2: Personal Growth Through Career Pivots
Introduction: Explore the journey of Alex, an IT professional who experienced substantial personal growth by navigating career pivots.
Elaboration:
- Strategies Employed:
  Alex proactively sought new challenges, transitioning between roles and industries to align his career with his evolving passions. He engaged in continuous learning, acquiring new skills that empowered his professional versatility.
- Challenges Overcome:
  Each career pivot presented unique challenges, from adjusting to

new work environments to overcoming imposter syndrome. Alex addressed these hurdles through resilience, mentorship, and a commitment to lifelong learning.
- Lessons Learned:
Alex's journey highlights the transformative power of embracing change and seeking personal growth through professional evolution. His story encourages individuals to view career shifts not as setbacks but as opportunities for development and fulfillment.

Narrative 3: The Pursuit of Work-Life Harmony
Introduction: Meet Emily, a project manager who prioritized work-life harmony, recognizing that balance might not always mean equal time allocation.
Elaboration:
- Strategies Employed:
Emily focused on aligning her professional and personal pursuits with her values, recognizing that harmony could be achieved by prioritizing activities that brought fulfillment. She implemented efficient time management strategies, allocating dedicated periods for both work and personal endeavors.
- Challenges Overcome:
The challenge for Emily lay in overcoming societal expectations around the traditional definition of balance. By emphasizing harmony, she navigated external pressures and carved a path that resonated with her aspirations.
- Lessons Learned:
Emily's story emphasizes the importance of redefining balance to align with one's unique circumstances and goals. Her pursuit of harmony showcases that equilibrium can be achieved by intentionally integrating various aspects of life based on individual priorities.

Implementation and Audience:

These real-life stories serve as inspirational blueprints for individuals seeking to achieve a balance between their professional and personal lives while fostering personal growth. Readers looking to redefine their approach to balance, navigate career transitions, or prioritize work-life harmony will find valuable insights and practical strategies in these narratives. The implementation of the lessons drawn from these stories involves a conscious assessment of individual values, flexible adaptation to change, and a commitment to continuous learning.

Conclusion

- Key takeaways from each productivity hack
- Reinforcing the importance of planning

Conclusion: Key Takeaways for Time Mastery

As we wrap up this guide, let's distill the timeless insights from the ten productivity hacks, ensuring their relevance for years to come. Each hack represents a valuable tool contributing to the broader goal of mastering time and enhancing productivity. Let's explore the enduring lessons from each hack:

GoalGetter:
- Set ambitious yet achievable goals.
- Embrace habit tracking for sustained progress.
- Celebrate wins and conduct regular reviews for continuous improvement.

Daily Doen:
- Prioritize comprehensive daily planning.
- Balance work and personal tasks for holistic productivity.
- Integrate gratitude journaling for a positive mindset.

Visionary:
- Utilize the vision board feature for goal visualization.
- Engage in long-term planning for realizing grand ideas.
- Embrace abundant space for fostering creativity.

Wellness Warrior and Mindful Maven:
- Track health and wellness for overall well-being.
- Encourage healthy habits and mindfulness exercises.
- Cultivate a mindful lifestyle for a serene life.

Time Titan, Taskmaster, and Efficiency Expert:
- Implement time blocking for focused efficiency with Time Titan.
- Utilize task prioritization strategies with Taskmaster.
- Streamline tasks and boost productivity with Efficiency Expert.

Balance Builder and Reflection Rookie:
- Achieve work-life equilibrium with Balance Builder.
- Foster personal growth through reflection and goal setting with Reflection Rookie.

Synthesizing Timeless Insights:

This section synthesizes the enduring insights from each productivity hack, emphasizing their interconnected nature. Readers are encouraged to recognize the synergies between different hacks, tailoring their approach to time management based on personal preferences and objectives. These timeless takeaways underscore the versatility of these tools in transforming one's relationship with time.

Empowering Readers Across Years:

The goal is to empower readers with a timeless understanding of diverse productivity methodologies. By internalizing these key takeaways, individuals can create a personalized productivity toolkit that aligns with their unique needs and aspirations, regardless of the year.

Implementation Guidance:

The conclusion not only highlights what has been learned but also provides practical guidance on implementing these timeless insights. Readers will discover how to seamlessly integrate these productivity hacks into their lives, fostering a sustainable and transformative approach to time management.

As we conclude this evergreen journey, remember that mastering time is an ongoing process. The key takeaways serve as a foundation for continuous growth, offering a roadmap for readers to navigate the complexities of their personal and professional lives with efficiency, purpose, and fulfillment. In the final section of the conclusion, we'll reinforce the fundamental importance of planning for enduring productivity.

Reinforcing the Importance of Planning

In the grand tapestry of productivity, planning stands as the masterstroke that weaves together the threads of time, goals, and accomplishments. As we delve into the significance of planning, it's crucial to emphasize its perpetual importance, transcending the boundaries of a specific year. Let's reinforce this timeless principle:

1. Strategic Navigation:

- Planning serves as the compass that directs us through the vast landscape of our ambitions. It provides a roadmap, allowing us to navigate through the complexities of our personal and professional spheres with intention and purpose.
- Strategic planning involves setting clear objectives, identifying potential challenges, and charting a course that aligns with our overarching goals. It's a proactive approach that minimizes the likelihood of drifting aimlessly and maximizes the chances of reaching our desired destinations.

2. Goal Alignment:

- Effective planning ensures that our daily, weekly, and monthly activities align seamlessly with our long-term goals. It bridges the gap between envisioning the future and living in the present moment.
- By continually reassessing and refining our plans, we maintain a dynamic connection between our immediate actions and the larger narrative of our aspirations. This alignment enhances our focus, making every effort a deliberate step toward the fulfillment of our overarching vision.

3. Adaptive Resilience:

- Planning is not a rigid structure but a flexible framework that accommodates the twists and turns of life. It instills adaptive resilience, allowing us to respond thoughtfully to unforeseen circumstances and changing priorities.
- As we reinforce the importance of planning, it's crucial to highlight the adaptive nature of effective planning. It's not about creating an inflexible agenda but about cultivating the ability to pivot, adjust, and recalibrate our plans as needed.

4. Time Optimization:

- At its core, planning is a potent tool for optimizing our most precious resource: time. It compels us to evaluate the significance of each task, prioritize effectively, and allocate our time where it matters most.
- Reinforcing the importance of planning involves recognizing time as a finite asset and acknowledging that intentional planning is the key to extracting maximum value from every moment.

5. Holistic Well-being:

- Beyond professional pursuits, planning extends its influence into our personal lives, contributing to holistic well-being. It prompts us to allocate time for self-care, leisure, and meaningful connections.
- Reinforcing the importance of planning entails recognizing its role in crafting a balanced and fulfilling life, where both personal and professional dimensions coexist harmoniously.

Practical Integration:

The conclusion not only emphasizes the significance of planning but also provides practical insights on integrating planning seamlessly into our lives. Readers will find actionable tips on creating effective plans, incorporating flexibility, and cultivating a planning mindset that endures across time.

In summary, as we reinforce the importance of planning, we are championing a timeless principle that transcends the temporal boundaries of a specific year. Planning is the perennial companion on our journey to mastery over time, guiding us with unwavering relevance through the ever-evolving landscapes of our lives.

Appendix

- Glossary of technical terms
- Additional resources for further reading

Appendix

Glossary of Technical Terms

To enhance your understanding of the concepts discussed throughout this book, here's a comprehensive glossary of technical terms used across various chapters:

Productivity:
- *Definition:* The measure of efficiency in completing tasks and achieving goals within a given timeframe.

Time Management:
- *Definition:* The systematic organization and prioritization of tasks to optimize the use of time.

Planners:
- *Definition:* Tools designed to assist individuals in organizing tasks, setting goals, and managing their time effectively.

GoalSetter:
- *Definition:* A person who actively engages in setting and achieving goals.

Daily Doen:
- *Definition:* A planner that focuses on detailed daily planning, balancing work and personal tasks.

Visionary Planner:
- *Definition:* A planner with features like vision boards, emphasizing long-term planning and fostering creativity.

Wellness Warrior:
- *Definition:* A planner focused on tracking health and wellness, encouraging healthy habits.

Mindful Maven:
- *Definition:* A planner that promotes mindful living through exercises and self-care reminders.

Time Titan:
- *Definition:* A planner emphasizing time blocking as a technique for efficiency.

Taskmaster:
- *Definition:* A planner that prioritizes tasks effectively, distinguishing between urgent and important.

Efficiency Expert:
- *Definition:* A planner equipped with tips and tricks to streamline tasks, optimize time, and boost overall productivity.

Balance Builder:
- *Definition:* A planner focusing on achieving a harmonious work-life equilibrium.

Reflection Rookie:
- *Definition:* A planner designed for personal growth and reflection, featuring sections for self-reflection, goal setting, and progress tracking.

SMART Goals:
- *Definition:* A goal-setting framework emphasizing Specific, Measurable, Achievable, Relevant, and Time-bound criteria.

Batch Processing:
- *Definition:* A technique where similar tasks are grouped and completed consecutively to minimize mental effort.

Two-Minute Rule:
- *Definition:* A principle suggesting that tasks taking two minutes or less should be completed immediately.

Automation Tools:
- *Definition:* Software or tools that handle repetitive tasks automatically.

Delegation Strategies:
- *Definition:* Methods for distributing tasks effectively among team members or collaborators.

Feel free to refer to this glossary whenever you encounter these terms to deepen your comprehension of the content.

Note: This glossary provides concise definitions, but if you seek a more detailed explanation or have additional questions, consider referring to the respective chapters for contextual insights.

Now, let's explore the second section of the Appendix, which includes additional resources for further reading.

Additional Resources for Further Reading

Congratulations on completing your guide to enhanced productivity and time management! To further support your journey toward improved efficiency and personal development, consider exploring the following resources:

Books:
- *Atomic Habits by James Clear:* Dive into the science of habit formation to understand how small changes can lead to remarkable results.
- *Getting Things Done by David Allen:* Explore a comprehensive system for improving productivity and organizing tasks.
- *Deep Work by Cal Newport:* Learn about the benefits of deep, focused work and strategies for cultivating it in a distracted world.

Online Courses:
- *Coursera:* Explore courses on time management, productivity, and personal development from top universities and organizations.
- *LinkedIn Learning:* Access a variety of courses on productivity, leadership, and efficiency to further enhance your skills.
- *Udemy:* Find practical courses on goal setting, time management, and efficiency to apply in your daily life.

Podcasts:
- *The Tim Ferriss Show:* Listen to interviews with successful individuals as they share insights on productivity, habits, and life optimization.
- *The Productivity Show by Asian Efficiency:* Gain practical tips and strategies for improving your productivity and achieving your goals.
- *Optimal Living Daily:* Enjoy daily readings of the best blogs on personal development, productivity, and self-improvement.

Websites and Blogs:
- *Lifehacker:* Stay updated on the latest tips and hacks for improving various aspects of your life.
- *Zen Habits by Leo Babauta:* Explore minimalist and mindful approaches to productivity and personal development.
- *The Muse:* Access a wealth of articles on career development, productivity, and work-life balance.

Apps:
- *Todoist:* A task management app that helps you organize and prioritize your to-do list.
- *Forest:* Enhance your focus and reduce distractions by growing a virtual forest while working.

- *Headspace:* Incorporate mindfulness and meditation into your routine for improved well-being.

These resources cover a range of topics related to productivity, time management, and personal development. Remember to tailor your approach to what works best for you and enjoy the ongoing journey of self-improvement!

Feel free to explore these resources at your own pace, and may they contribute to your continuous growth and success. Thank you for being part of this transformative journey.